W9-ABY-177

House of Poured-Out Waters   *

HOUSE OF
POURED-OUT WATERS

Poems by Jane Mead

University of Illinois Press

Urbana and Chicago

Library of Congress Cataloging-in-Publication Data
Mead, Jane, 1958–
House of poured-out waters : poems / by Jane Mead.
p.   cm.
ISBN 0-252-02644-6 (cloth : alk. paper)
ISBN 0-252-06944-7 (pbk. : alk. paper)
I. Title.
PS3563.E165H68   2001
811'.54—dc21   00-010688

1 2 3 4 5 C P 5 4 3 2 1

ACKNOWLEDGMENTS

Grateful acknowledgement is due the magazines and anthologies in which the following poems first appeared, sometimes in different versions.

"The Future," "The Animal Messenger," "To Break the Spell Is to Invite Chaos into the Universe," "But What If, as Is," "Lack, the Willow," and "Lack, the Hummingbird" appeared in *American Poetry Review*.

Ten sections from "Several Scenes in Search of the Same Explosion" appeared in *Bellingham Review*.

"Problem Performed by Shadows" appeared in *Beloit Poetry Journal*.

"The Prairie as Valid Provider" appeared on-line in *Caffeine Destiny*.

"Talking to You" appeared in *Colorado Review*.

"Notes toward a Definition" appeared in *Indiana Review*.

"However," and "What Happens" appeared in *Iowa Review*.

"The Seventh Revelation of My Thirty-Seventh Year" appeared in *Luna*.

"I Have Been Living" appeared in the *New York Times*.

"Point of Departure," "The Ring around the Reappearing Body," and "House of Poured-Out Waters" appeared in *Pequod*.

"And All These Things Are So" appeared in *Ploughshares*.

"Rather" appeared in *Poetry Flash*.

"Wind" appeared in *Shenandoah*.

"Rather a Pale Occasion for Flowers" and "Incomplete Scenario Involving What the Voice Said" appeared in *Sonora Review*. "Incomplete Scenario Involving What the Voice Said" also appeared in *Bread Loaf Anthology of New American Poets*.

"The World" appeared in *TriQuarterly*.

I am grateful to the Patrick Lannan Foundation for the Completion Grant that afforded me the time in which to finish this collection.

For their friendship, their unwavering faith in these poems, and their painstaking help with this collection, my thanks to Ira Sadoff, Timothy Liu, Dennis Sampson, Tess Gallagher, Christine Garren, and Jan Weissmiller.

My thanks as well to my colleagues in the English Department at Wake Forest University for their invaluable support and flexibility.

For Parry and for Whit—
For my mother

Do the bones cast out their fire?

—Theodore Roethke, "The Lost Son"

CONTENTS

5

TO BREAK THE SPELL IS TO INVITE
CHAOS INTO THE UNIVERSE

It would be easier
if I did not exist—

but I did. It would be
easier if there were

nothing left, but there is—
mementos weeded down to

how to miss the out-juttings
below the cliff, ocean

behind all the doors and windows.
Ocean,—and the watery sky.

On the cliff-face the swallow
is making her home of mud and feathers.

Out of mud and feathers
she makes a home.

Earth or music?

The music as the earth: just so:
The horizon beyond the horizon—.

THE FUTURE

As a child, who you were
was located in the future—

right? Now where is
your existence. In

there were dogs—
then we buried them?

Berries, so we put them
in jars? There were

guns, so we fired them
at one another, or didn't—.

Just as the scene was predicted?
Just as the act was forewritten?

RATHER

Rather, we must begin
way before here. To believe
is not so easy. *Paragraph
after paragraph of rain*
was the right thing.

There are children standing
like numb pigeons
in every paragraph—
just watching us.

See, they were not bees at all.
Instead—we are responsible for them.

We said, *sunlit passages
we can't describe,* we said,
blackout. We said,
put out the fiasco.

They said, *we are the fiasco.*

We never said *children* once.

They stood in the heavy downpour,
paragraph after paragraph,

their true mittens hanging from their sleeves—
little red embassies.

5

AND ALL THESE THINGS ARE SO

If the trees are alive
and I am alive,
if the trees are blazing,

and the seagull—flying
between the grass and sun—
makes a shadow,

if the sky startles me,
if my soul is listening, waiting
for something to fly

from the bony cage of my hands—
then how can it be,
how *can* it be, that when I raise them

and make the motions of blossoming
they are empty?

LACK, THE OWL

Look early, look late.
Look up to fate —
magnify the moment.

Get the gist of it —
magnify the gist of it. —
Where the owl complains.

The owl in the night, complaining.
Who said he speaks to you?
Who said he speaks into night?

Who said he complains.
Define an act of betrayal?
Define an act of faith.

Magnify the moment.
Too much like a wing?
Too much like a shadow?

Too much like fate. —
Exercise the owl sound.
Repel doubt.

Too early. Too late.

remaining central, there is
some knowledge we do not
debate: a child is born

to his body the day he is
born, for example, or
the sky's felt time

seems like mourning:
the grasshoppers are anonymous
to the anonymous, the birds

are always at attendance.
There comes a moment
when you see as the crow sees:

the body as slaughterhouse,
as beggar — in the long grass, kneeling.

BUT WHAT IF, AS IS

often the case, it takes
months, years even, for that
specific tree to finish
falling, and furthermore

all during that time
lots of birds nest
in that tree, and the tree
and the birds call *each other*

into existence, mutually,—
meaning what if we really
aren't the center of
our spectacularly uncentered

universe but, rather, the tree,
the sound of it falling is what
calls us forth, and then here it is,
taking months, years even—

beginning with its creaking
in the *whispering wind*, working
up to the tiniest of crackings—
and then another patient waiting

for the song of eleven strong
rains, a magic number of fogs
and a certain added heaviness
of moss, until finally, and right

between two of the smallest
units of time (the size of which
of course do not exist, yet are
hauled back now for this occasion

from the land where a duck set out
across a pond and was left
in eternal exhaustion to his own
personal so-close-but-yet-so-far)

what if, that is, it's months
before the split tree splits
a little farther (twice as far,
exactly say, as the first split)

and it does this splitting almost
soundlessly, save for a branch
that hits its neighbor's branch,
sounding like a distant .22,

and what if the *decisive* crack
will come in a future emptied
completely of the likes of us
(*by* the very likes of us)

yet, still, I *am* here now, near that
aforementioned and graceless
shifting, and it takes me
back to the guns of my childhood—

and what if I want *that* to count,
that little crack, so that the memory
now, and therefore the childhood,
are called with me into existence,

meaning back into existence,
and another memory tags along,
for it is a part of that same
childhood, the memory of imagining

a tree and a forest in order to give
some life to a question—couldn't it
all add up, the trees, the moss,
the puny cracking, to me,—

existing, every atom of me,
so that I might have this chance
to ask you (who are a problem
for another day) what brand

of confusion it would take
for what manner of pervert to ask
that particular question
of a potentially invisible child?

LACK, THE MEMORY

Remember the door?
    I remember the door.

Remember the door and the wall.
    I remember the wall.

The wall and the Smith and Wesson?
    The hand blackened by gunpowder.

I remember the weeping.
    And I remember the door.

But most of all there were iris.
    Inside and outside.

And amaryllis in the kitchen.
    The door—left open for the cat.

Left open for the rain.
    And the ghosts passing through.

Remember the hinges?
    I remember the door and the hinges.

Remember the sky?
    And the ragged clouds within.

Think of the worlds within them.
    I remember the one world.

From before or after?
    From before.

From before the gunpowder?
    From before.

So what was the last thing?
    A face—cleansed by grief.

A face, cleansed by grief, in a dream.

THE ANIMAL MESSENGER

The loon call happens
on the marsh now, the marsh
rainbowed with oil—colors

of a chosen landscape,
purples and greens against
the tans and grays of fall

falling into winter.
The loon call happens and happens—
ripples outward, colorless

and shocked, and nowhere
meeting with a love of life
to make it certain.

TALKING TO YOU

*

Night and I'm a chromosome,
spinning.
Rats chew the floorboards.

Day, and I defect.
Roots pushing through the foundation —
ivy, some leaves too, under
my desk in the basement.

Sunlight stutters into this world
bringing another world with it. —

But light's just a question
I'm living through —
banner for the yellow bird,
white flag for the backward word.

Lots of work to be done here. I'm
making flypaper out of history.
—Personal *and* cultural.
—Remember that.

Daylight changes all the answers.
Daylight tries to.

Bars on the window.
Dog on the desk looks through them.
Sometimes she barks, a disintegration
of its own kind—but she loves me.

*

When I get through with drinking
maybe I'll tell you how
sun's a shattering I held onto,
maybe say it some way
you can make use of, maybe.

—Meanwhile, bed's the place
I go home to, and the eerie light
called daylight and the weaker light
that makes the night a vision.

How about *you* tell *me* a story?

Make it to do with the fate of the earth,
start with the world's beginning.
Maybe you could mention
my name—or just say *Julie*.

Then say it's the same
for how I love her.

—The god that is in me
is the god that is in her.

Where do *you* go home to?

*

Lots of work to be done here.
Have you noticed?

My father is a brilliant drunk.
Mutters to himself loudly,
and in public. At best.

I saw my mother laugh once —
most everybody else missed it,
but I say I saw it and I saw.

I myself wanted to live here.
With you.
Sane as a monkey
with someplace to go.

I've done my share of sweeping,
but am erratic.
And unforgivable.

This much I know:
If you start with loss
you go nowhere, and if
you start with nowhere
you start here.

The visions of the day return
as the visions of the night.
And stay.

Call me.

*

Meanwhile, phone unplugged
with a motion as fell
and unspecific as moonlight—
means *you* that is.

When I get through with drinking,
when I get through with thinking,
going to lay this body down—
sleep like something you might get.

Did I say that there's a god
within me?

And if I did, in what
dark corner of your mind
did you then tuck me?

The more I seek the source
of this divinity,
farther I get from time,
farther *you* are from mine.

Where *do* you go home to?

Do you miss me?

*

Because you'll never guess
this rage is love—
I have to tell you:
One glance and I'm with you—
want to dance?

In this way we'll begin
another story,
and it has another side:
One false move and

Damn straight I know
where I'm going.

You should throw your life away
and try it.

*

This is my only story.
I wouldn't trade it
for anything.

Not for a thing.

Do you hear me?
Do you understand?

Daylight resembles the day.
I resemble the sky.
I resemble a glass of water.

I do not think we choose —

night, and I'm a chromosome,
spinning. Days it deepens —

hair plastered to my forehead.
In the end, all I wanted to say
was this: *marrow deep,*
Sweet Jesus how I'm singing.

You should peel your skin off
and hear me.

SEVERAL SCENES IN SEARCH OF THE SAME EXPLOSION

+
What I want is
for them to say, to be
able to say, "They
wept well, they sang."

Of us all, and
whoever *they* will be,
in whatever language
speaking: "From

antiquity to their
brooding capsize,
they sang well—*duende*
in their fists, fire

in their feet, dust
of glass in their veins."

+

River mud between my toes
and I can tell you this:
the four dogs have
their four pure joys—

mud on their whiskers,
slime to their knees.
Milk-Bones in my pockets,
kennel up on the

dark of my tongue,
and I save it—though the
house behind the brambles
wants me. *Because*

the house behind
the brambles wants me.
Leon, in prison,
made the plaque that's

hanging in the kitchen:
Home, Sweet Home—
etched on mirror,
brambles of roses

and roses wreathed
around the centered words.

+

Clapboard, sheets on the line—
just what I want, just as
Leon, out now, wants me
to believe his hand,

half-raised again in anger,
can be lowered—*half*
raised: moment erased
by moment. Half

believing: mind
erased by the mind.
True sheets snapping
behind me now,

not like gunshot, but
like gunshot muffled
by the mind (moment
made over) and what

use is it—you sing, and then
you hear the words, you
accompany the scene, it
goes abstract: smudge of green

for river grass, streak
of red for the river and a
greenish wash of air
for sky: blur of pretty

colors with a title: *landscape
with house in distance.*

+
And you can have the what
it all leads back to,
and you can have
this story: the man

who was a terror is the
terror in the wheelchair:
red flag on a pole
against his back means

stand to the side of the hall,
press your body
against the wall, keep
eyes on your reflection,

how it ripples on the
polished floor. Comic flag.
Coming down to, comes
down to *you can have it—*

how he wants to play chess now,
wants to remember the day,
twenty years ago, or so,
but anyway *ago*, my mother

setting up the pieces wrong
then beating him, and how
he needs to say it:
"And I never beat her again."

Then, "But that was
unfortunate wording." And
then he says it again—
"That was unfortunate wording."

What value shall we assign
his fantasy, his repetition?

+

Or maybe I came back
to discover what the river means,
how to read *that* love—
mosquitoes purring

on the dense banks, gnats
in the sticker-leaf, maggots
in the loam, and the dome
of canopy holding the world in,

holding it out (keeping it green)—
because I'm here too, in the
reflected air, with a
log, or a stone from under

for a face—and I need
the river for that reflection.

+

The story of my cowardice
goes like this: what I
tell him: tell him how
I remember that year

as the year he taught me
chess, snow coming down,
fire in the fireplace,
the year of the Christmas

he gave me the woolen jacket
with the little house
embroidered on the back,
pinks and greens so lovely

I never wore it—when there was
also the dimple in the
dining-room floor, place
where the bullet didn't

enter flesh, and cat-howls
in the distance—sucked
back from their conclusion,
which was their origin. Which

is: my sister on the porch
lumped on the ice where
he threw her in the
days before his wheelchair.

Mom at the stove, stirring
and frying, me in the rocker,
singing, while we wait for the
final explosion, the one

that will carry us finally all down
into the dark — at last.

+

Never comes. Comes
only the moment when you
have to go on, get up
look for the flashlight

in the tool drawer, the moment
when you break the scene:
you break the tune, you
risk your body because

she has a sister. That
is the only moment
left you, the moment you
can go back to. Isn't it

home now? Waiting for the
kindling point, and it's
hard to explain the marriage
of desperation and courage

but what if you had to
defend *yourself* now,
that one you gave away —
remember? There's a line

beyond which what is real
is real and if I could
live on the other side
I would know how to live.

Oil on water. Sunlight on oil.
Answer that doesn't answer.

+

Can the meaning of this river lie
in how the banks do not
define it? How it's moving
under the reflected world, swollen

as if the whole of life lay
ahead, sluggish but there, under
the sheen of a surface—ripple
in the mind's eye, moment

swept under, then
rising and spreading—thinning?

+

The story of my cowardice
goes like this: broken bottle
against your throat, *my* throat—
the *then* so that now

when he tells me to find him
something yellow I wheel the chair
over to the window, lift
the binoculars and find

the early leaf shoots
of some gnarled tree, green,
with a yellowish wash,
which I point out though

I'll never know if this
is the kind of yellow
that will do, only that a
small swift bird, true yellow,

shoots out of the lenses'
circle just as I steady it—
just as the world offers it, not
a symbol, not a promise,

just a glimmer. Or
goes like this: glimmer
that I fail
to mention. Or like this:

I bring iris. I
bring roses, scan for yellow.

+

Canopy keeping the
world green, banks gone
soggy where the river
flooded. For how long

shall I hide my face, tell me,
for it is ugly because it
knows something larger
than it fathoms, answers

to something brutal
and elsewhere that tastes
like the river and the
leaves in the gully.

Rabbit in the clearing, back
facing to me, dogs off
barking down a false
trail and I look

away and when I look back
she's still there, making
a silhouette, ears big
like in the comics, serious—

like in the comics.
And I look away because if
she's still there when I
look again, I am free

or lost, or a woman
standing by a river—
waiting and spitting to
scare her out: the *what*

it is that she means,
and meaning to last out
the dusk before looking.
What value shall we assign

the blur of her reflection?
Gardez, check, checkmate.

\+

Lines of brambles webbing
my face and I
can go into the hour
of whatever I'll

give back—my thinness
and my shyness: nothing
but how I keep him, keep
you, from hurting me, body

as baggage, waiting
for music or a deeper shade
of dark to jolt it loose. Meanwhile,
Leon, and house in distance—

slime between my toes
where the river receded,
eyes averted, waiting
out the dusk, not looking—

mind patching colors
the world gives back—wanting
not to have to name it: *this*:
my banner, my white flag? You can do

anything to me, and in the end,
if I love you I will love you?

+

You start some-
where, you
start because you
have to, you

climb without
knowing you climb,
you arrive without
knowing where

you are, and when
you fall there is
no difference
between the dark

and the light
and what you know.

+

So that this is not
about love anymore,
but about the body
in the song, broken

and free—a loss
like the trench of
real sky where the river
clears it: world

of blue falling
into world of black,
out in the outer
hemispheres where we

cannot see it—looking
up, sounds like weeping,
like *yes*, swells like
singing—rabbit thumping

out the beat, but who
can hear her—just the sound
of twigs snapping. Shards
of glass in bank-light,

light on a river, river
in my veins, blood in my
throat, leaves on my tongue.
About how I say it—

none of you
will ever own me, ever.

3　✳

RATHER A PALE OCCASION FOR FLOWERS

It never was—the way you remember.
You'd zero in on fog, say, when really
what was memorable about the place
was the cacti: and you all this while
intent on how fast the wind
could carry a waft of fog on by.

Certainly, there is fire in your hair.
But when I speak of it you just say
rain, child, fireplace—as I remember
we cooked a lot and even now
with the stone lions waving at the end
of the driveway, with the five ginkgoes
safely installed, and neither cacti nor fog
in the forecast, there is most merely
the sensed presence of buds—
just as not long ago there was
the mere sensed presence of snow.

Even so—with or without your wanting—
the day wants on: tulips rise, crows
make a vision of the lemon tree.

—And all with a wash of nightmare
wafting through. So: you bark, you growl,
you stick out your tongue, you lie
about praying, and you are never
in any shape to drive. Nevertheless
you take the car right through the flower stand
and on into the Mississippi. No matter.
There are other issues to attend to:
how the ugly child is thought to be
more dishonest than his cute peers,
or the presidential *search we high,*
search we low—no hanky. Do they suppose
we can mop up this much blood
with our french bread? This is all
an experiment in human nonsense,—
this, our symphony of frailty.

Self-mutilation, says Dr. John Briere,
is merely the attempt not *to commit*
suicide. You warning, you cursed flower you—
walk and keep on walking. Give yourself
a dog. There is this story the body
is trying to write—and you off
creating a fate-filled portrait of the day:
(eight ball, twenty cents, goodwill): *maybe,*
yes, definitely no . . . ask again later.

Rather a pale occasion for flowers
I'd say, but there is no known way
to hit on the random urge that is you, *being*.

Instead, you try this, you try that,
but every year, on the Fourth of July—
try as you might to avoid it—you end up
on the LEGALIZE POT float,
waving. We shall all move back now
one square with a single cheer
for how it happens. You see it never was
the way you remember, just an idea
shaping itself into time before
departing. You even made up the lions
because their waving was sufficient
to keep you going—though barely.

So, stand to. This isn't the scene
where you flatten the rear of the squirrel,
it's the instant after, the instant before
you hit reverse and back back over the body.

POINT OF DEPARTURE

(108th at the Hudson)

Could be anything, but it's pigeons:
taking off from the sides of buildings
and heading on out like an idea
that knows where it's going—beginning,
say, with the artsy part, then moving
downward, at an angle, toward whatever
a river might be reduced to after
it's been stripped of all its meaning.

Christ, they've been loaded and unloaded
to death, but I can start with *pretty* now—
start with rivers of pigeons, a pigeon-gray
river and miles of river-gray sky—
because I know I'm going to take it back soon,
and that something in the angle we've got going here,
how we're moving through it, or maybe just
caught in it, is what's going to save us,
keep us from stalling in mid-air.

Could have been anything, but it was
pigeons came to stand for what a sense
of *beautiful*, or *order* might do to a life, i.
e.—ruin it, like thinking in place of
a bird enacting the eating of crumbs.

Not a bird, not a net: it's nothing, that thought.
So, now we've got a scene that's lost its meaning—
which is the meaning we're bent on losing.

We want the common arc a common pigeon makes
with his wing-tips when he's moving, how it's
something like a tunnel you could live in
if you could turn as he turns, not lose the path
in thinking *wing-tips like a quick note repeating*
"If you can keep me, keep me," or how *a life could*
make that kind of room by moving through it.

To follow in that tunnel, stay right behind him.
Take nothing with you. However far you get,
go farther. Rest and then go farther.

Point in the direction of Harlem,
of Soho, or of Sutton, point
in the direction of Kansas—four
ways to water, to whoever you will be
when you arrive there, which is not
whatever you think you might imagine, but more
like that idea that knows where it's going
but keeps the plan of action to itself.

This is off the beaten track of how
you must pick up your cross and keep on lurching.

Point toward Harlem, be running—
NO RADIO, NO STEREO, NO CASSETTE, NOTHING
OF VALUE but the brutal windows
of a church in sunlight, but the little islands
that are the hopeless, and how I'm not the one
to help you with that image, to burden you,
unburden you, or hope to make your mind up
concerning the issue of dust and ashes.

You can do whatever you want now.
Do whatever you want. You can
move up Broadway repeating a tune
from the airways, staying dressed, not
breaking windows—whistling and avoiding arrest.

You can walk and keep on walking.
You can walk and arrive at water.
However far you get, go farther.
You are as free as you will ever be.
You are off the beaten track
of how you might not get there,
and you can mark the distance now in inches.

WIND

shaking the night loose.

The bay tree
by the pump-house door rattles.

The bones
of the pepper tree
rattle.

Do the heifers, then,
still balance on the hillside?

Are the iris which
crowd the meadows lost then?

Buds nipped by cold?

Brambles snap in the driveway.

WHAT HAPPENS

if you can't imagine yourself
anywhere — what then?

For example: here — who is going
to polish the candlesticks? Who

is going to light the beeswax candles
when darkness begins to enter

these woods and all you can think of
is how light leaves the prairie:

darkness doesn't come in. *Prairie,*
keep me going a little longer.

LACK, THE HUMMINGBIRD

Too early, too late:
lacking in faith—
unable to function.

Skip the hummingbird—
watch the hovering.
Watch with a mighty faith.

Say the sky's malleable.
Save the bird.
Too early, too late—.

Lacking in faith?
Unable to function?
Unable to pray.

Regard the space in the sky.
Encircle the hover.
Maneuver around the malfunction?

Too early, too late—
left up to faith.
Left up to fate—.

Too early, too late?

INCOMPLETE SCENARIO INVOLVING
WHAT THE VOICE SAID

The sky that is the limit is the one
sky—the moon: the same. Meanwhile,
back at the literal ranch, my father

is behind the barn boiling a cougar's
head. He does this for *my* love
of skulls, my love of how the curves

and arches hold. It is his birthday.
We speak by fax. I myself have been
out back picking up the frozen bodies

of birds while the thermometer
rises—perhaps sufficiently. In my
dream all the houses burn—but the people

are rescued. In reality, if the past
were a fence it would be what
they call *goat-high and hog-tight.*

And behind us. No turning back.
The year my father left us I
was six. I washed my clothes in The Muddy

Truckee all that summer—stripped
and sank them into the deep shore, then
tugged them out of the claylike mud

and waved them around in the current.
Meanwhile, my mother was working on becoming
a resident of the great state of

Nevada. There are, after all, only
so many strategies available—meaning
who ever heard of the moon as limit?—meaning

the sky, when all is said and done,
that is the limit, is the one sky, meaning
root hog, as they say on the farm, *or die.*

THE RING AROUND THE
REAPPEARING BODY

To speak of losing the F and AM waves
in the two tunnels by the Golden Gate
could be to mean if you can't bear your children's
voices, you put the children in the cellar.

But I would rather lead you to the cows
outside Stornetta's Dairy in Sonoma
who leave their calves with one heifer
and spend the day off grazing.

Still, you could get to the cows either way:
via the children and the cellar—via *that thought*—
or just by knowing how the road runs.
You could get there even with a map.

—Now, the fact is I was driving
in the other direction: my thoughts move
backward sometimes. I confess,
I am not completely in control.

But try this, if you trust me—
try to trust me—
I arrived in San Francisco early
and found a place for coffee. Simple.

The girls at the table next to mine
were faking the experiment: "Shall we write
that he moved less in the heat
even though we didn't do that part?"

Then, "Say the hairless mouse didn't get as hot,"
which struck me because I was reading
about a boy named Patrick in a Hampstead nursery—
we're in World War II now, and Patrick is singing.

Because he knows his mother
will not be coming back he's repeating
the same song over and over, and this,
I quote directly, is what he sings:

She will put on my overcoat and leggings,
she will zip up the zipper,
she will put on my pixie hat.

Some things, it seems, can't be abandoned,
because later, when they asked him
if he couldn't just shut up—only nicely—
he mimed his story in the corner.

They didn't have to look
at the zipping of the zipper, watch
the careful lowering down
of the hat, and so they didn't.

Funny, how it all veers back now
to the cellar I made up
for the sake of argument—or was it
for the sake of something truer?

Isn't this the part that matters? How it's not
just the story, or even how you read it—
kid wants his mother back, perhaps—
but how it travels, *that* it travels?

—How the story wasn't all he had: there was
also that saying it kept him with them.
Never mind how little they wanted him.
Never mind how he stood for loss.

—Never mind the dubious birth
of the hairless mouse, or the many roads
from Sonoma to the Golden Gate. Isn't desire,
for all its perversity, worth it?

I, for one, am sorry they lost him
because of how his rhythm rings—it's
the ring around the reappearing body—
and because he saved the pixie hat for last.

PROBLEM PERFORMED BY SHADOWS

Where the mind's eye comes together with the world
a woman is sleeping with her girlhood, the memory
of a dream dreamed by a stranger—by mistake

on a sunny afternoon in the back of his mind.
Mostly, he's shooting blue jays: when their shadows
meet their bodies, mind meets dream.

And the man who now cuts loose her dream
is the stranger from her woken world—
his headlights stain her bedroom wall with shadows:

deer heads on the woodpile mixing with memory,
shadows on a wall mixing in the mind,
two worlds intersecting as a single mistake.

She wants the blue jays to be killed by mistake.
She wants the shadows of deer heads to be dream.
She wants a world unstained by the mind—

but the world of shadows shadows the world
and the dream of the man is a man-made memory
and the memory is as simple as the shadow

of a man beating a woman, their single shadow
falling on the bedroom wall—a mistake.
She tells herself it is only a man as the memory

of a man, falling through the world to a wall in a dream.
The place where the shadow breaks in two is the world
she wants to get to, a place with space for the mind.

How they break, how they come together in the mind
is the problem performed by the shadows.
How it continues is the problem performed in the world.

In the house of adulthood she repeats the mistake
of jays from her girlhood who die when she dreams.
They enter their shadows with a thud—just a memory.

She thinks, *this the world, that the memory.*
She says *that the shadow, this the mind.*
The man drops his car keys on the dresser—*not a dream.*

Without headlights, the deer heads cast no shadows.
She pulls the years up around her, this mistake
is of her making—how he comes out of the world

into her dream could be a memory—a shadow
her mind let happen in the world by mistake.
She tells him she's been dreaming of the world.

4 *

HOUSE OF POURED-OUT WATERS

+
First there's the
one about the baby
in Boston whose mother
thought to fry him. You

may have read about it
in the papers, circa 1968—
yes, I was ten. Today,
he's a walking, talking

miracle, a monument to the
fine art of skin grafting.
The rest of us, meanwhile,
can relax—he's already

been reported, as in *to the*
Childhood Grief Center
(Minneapolis) (as in
to the Emergency

Room) . . . *(Society for the*
Prevention of Cruelty
to Children) . . . *(Hurricane*
Center) (I was joking)

(Somewhere in FL)
(a fact)—later to resurface
in the asylum, and, therefore,
to the folks in Minneapolis.

Relax. This is not his story.
I just wanted you to know.

+

Rather, what we're back to
is another take on the
saga in process—another
chapter in the story of

me and you—how what I want
is to give you something—
yes, you, via description,
and after my hot bath,

pen in hand and Mozart
on the tape machine, clean
and wanting to begin again
at yet another shoreline—

the beach as it was this morning,
dawn-fog, sun seeping through
from the unavailable background,
a world all shades of gold

and gray, their mixing
and their churning—a man
long dead providing the
score, *Exsultate, Jubilate*—

Can you hear it?
Do you want it?

\+

Because there's also
how he must have
suffered to know that
kind of beauty, though

I won't say that's
what suffering is
for—still if I could
truly make a note here

I'd shape it like a
footnote on the mother,
her hunger—maybe for
a scream to match the

scream inside her, maybe
for some final silence,
outer hemispheres sucking
the sounds in, as if

to make a path from
there to here: that
arc you've got to form
in your imagination if I'm

going to have something
left to trade for what
I want to know, since what
I want to know is this:

what would you want read
to you in the moment
before your final sleep?
We will gather around you,

we will read, by the light
of candles, in hushed voices.

\+

Or maybe it begins where
it always ends, maybe
it begins with the body,
my body—reappearing

like some kind of
refrain: I look down
and she's there again,
after all these years,

there because braced
in a doorframe between
a kitchen and a hall, between
children and father, paint

under her fingernails, and I
recognize her. Same globe
of too-bright light
fading the scene out, air

filling with the sounds
of human children,
weeping, then the sounds
of human anger—that

other kind of grieving—
room filling and
emptying like a great
and weary lung, heaving—

and she, in the doorway,
holding out for the space
between them, braced—
as if strung up.

I look down and
see her. I look down
and see how the rest
of her life is the rest

of my life. I ask her
to raise her eyes then, don't I.

+

I am speaking to you as a last resort.
I wanted to make a prayer.
I spent the youthful part
of a lifetime on it. It

did not read well. I moved
to be by the ocean—it's
where we came from, where we'll
go back to, after all, maybe

as ashes, maybe as flesh, maybe
as the one we didn't want to be—
the one who can be done without.
In my darker moments I

talk to the air. I pretend
you are here. This
is not presumption. Just
despair. There is blood

everywhere I go: in Safeway,
spurting across the rows
of Ajax, and the mother—blonde—
and the daughter—blonde—

wandering on by as if
nothing at all were happening.
Wherever I see them I imagine
the entrance of terror

in the specific form of a man
holding a broken bottle. It seems
I am about to witness the slaughter
but the truth is the blood

has already been spilled—
right before my mind
did the scene in. I have
some knowledge of the

basic theories of the psyche.
I have some grounding
in theories of the soul.
Everywhere I go there is blood—

no way to tell the darkness outside
from the darkness within.

+

Do you believe the colors
blind men in doorways
gesture to are real?
Sometimes I look up

and they are there, grays
and golds that are
churning—or only in that
(as in do you believe

only in that) world as a
clutter of clichés—not
just the forms in alleys
along the way, but the

way I'm trying to clear
some path right through them,
treading the thinning cusp
between knowing and

walking—understanding as the
famous booby prize, functioning
as some kind of trophy
I could perm my hair

and press a dress to collect—
then keep on washing up for—
sick with a knowledge
I can neither name

nor find the courage for, sick
with the choice I'll have
to make one fine day, sick
with fog, dawn-time, sky

shattered, sun trying, waves
trying—lovely for what
they are worth—all out beyond
the beachfront property, where

maybe it's all drifting together,
maybe all drifting apart.

+

Should have begun with the
angel in Central Park
(by Emma Stebbins, circa
1873). Do you know her? —

Feet caught in the
moment before she discovers
her weight, one hand
out for balance, wings

still full of air. Just
some metal made into
wings, just some wings
about to fold in, just

a statue, pigeons on her
head, Mozart on the
tape machine, vacuum
in the place where the

notes rise up (how he
must have suffered) life
from which something
beautiful was made, pen-in-hand

for how I want it, *Exsultate,*
Jubilate, words from elsewhere
seeping out of the unavailable
background: *though the world*

destroy this body, yet
in my flesh shall I
see God—sense of humor
standing for survival

Exsultate standing for
itself and for how
I want to hold it
out in the cup I make

of my bony hands,—
and how the cup won't hold it.

+

Dark and I come
to the note then that
almost breaks me before
it fades, clearing

the path to *elsewhere*
so I might ask you
kindly what I would
have asked in anger—

(the very least equaling
the very most here and we're
back to the angel in
Central Park and how I want

to know) if you can tell
by her face, utterly tragic,
utterly beautiful, that she
has been here before,

that *this* is the moment
of her final landing,
that she belongs to us now.
Angel at the pool of Bethez:

house of olives, house
of mercy, house of
poured-out waters,
and the story of a man

healed not with water
only, but with the water
and with the blood: rain
on metal, metal that's a

face, face that is true —
notes rising up toward
elsewhere, outer hemispheres
sucking the sound in. Then

from somewhere the coo
of pigeons. *How* elsewhere is it?

+

When I look at the photos
of Hedda, I see the one
I can't let happen. When I
look at the pictures

of Lisa I am loosed
on the world unfit, sense
of irony holding my
words together, wedge

of cruelty keeping me
human, lumbering
toward midnight-happening,
holding my fractured skull:

I may be landing,
I may be taking off—
all I want is to
give you something

before it happens, something
a person could live by.

+

Numb tongue, tongue
soaked in blood, thrumming
itself on the roof
of a mouth, sense of

humor flatter than the
Nimitz, flat place where
my life shook itself
apart, face down in the

dust, distance collapsing
under the weight of its
greatness—distance
between the life that is

yes and the life
that is *no*, ground-level
as the ever popular life
that is *maybe*. (Face down.)

Wanting something more
than how I said it—
*none of you will ever
own me, ever*—room of my

telling collapsing,
collapsing the space
for the place we have together.
And I wanted to give you something?

Something more than
how I said it: *Ever.*

+

I am only half-way home
but I know the things I know:
You do not destroy the ones
you hate, you only change them

into something you can do
without, something you think
you can do without. There is
a kind of freedom here,

a place I'm trying to get to—
lies with my only secret: how
when he wrenches his arm back
to slug you, what you do

is look in his eyes hard.
That look, the final betrayal—
and all you get back
is your body, blood on your

chin, tongue soaked in blood,
and a glimpse of where
you are trying to get to, place
that might finish you, place

that might save you, you
don't know—you just go
because it is where you
are going (wedge of sarcasm

keeping you sane, keeping you
distant). Distance how you
stay alive here. Boiling
down to nothing. Sometimes

it seems I am choking myself,
sometimes it seems I'm just choking.

+

Sometimes I mourn the
beach, woo the waves
out beyond the you-know-
what. At night when the

moonlight's trying to
keep us, I walk the rib
of shoreline speaking
to my soul, saying *soul,*

teach me how to dance
real slow, real quick—
just once before the moon
goes out and the lights

go down over Frisco. The
fog rolls in some more.
I hold whatever thought
I need to know it—I

hold whatever thought
might reel the soul in, I
hope they are the same
thought—I hold my

two arms out, say *soul,*
we will come to the one
o-happy end to our
defection, go endlessly

forward together—*sometimes*
we will call ourselves
beauty, *sometimes*
we will call ourselves

pain. *We will marry ourselves*
to the fate of the earth:
sky churning, waves
breaking, notes breaking.

Unavailable moonlight.
Acres of silence out beyond.

+
An arc that is inside
out is still an arc, the
path that leads to lightness
leads to dark: the stone

in New York that says
GOD'S ANGEL wants to mean
there was no such child
as Lisa Steinberg, means —

without wanting to — the
truth: there was only
Lisa, and she belonged
to us. I have carried

him for twenty-three years,
back curled over where he
hit the griddle, and I
hand him back now, and I

take him with me — silence
at the end of the tape receding.

NOTES TOWARD A DEFINITION

*

Maybe we start with the part about how
we embody the theory of dust
and ashes now, that pure place beyond
image and story and voice—*those* lies.

Maybe we start with the dark room,
you in it, skeletal, waiting, for the pieces—
not to come together even, but just to
surface—let us begin with Baudelaire:
Sorrow be wise, be calm and how
any old-time biker, any Person-In-Black,
any girl from the suburbs
with her head shaved bald could tell you—
there's no music in the background
that can help you.

For now I shall sleep in the dust
and thou shalt seek me in the morning
but I shall not be. That's Job.
And *this* is where you begin,
begin by blowing smoke on a bug
to move him without moving your knee,
and this part wants to leave a space
to overlap the moment when you'll notice —
now that you've numbed him in his tracks —
the white stripe on his wings, gold stripe
like eyeliner at its rim, and think
like eyeliner, but perfect. And all this
by the light of a cigarette.

*

What I meant to say about chaos theory
is that the important part is *not* the theory,
not even the chaos, but the mind, how it
lays itself down over century after century—
(*like eyeliner*, like *like*) and then
the obliging centuries—like a thought
saying *maybe it's the overlap of mind*
upon the centuries, the shape of which
is perfect—that part rising now, beyond your reach
regardless of how much you want it.
Then, *maybe it's a shadow.*

Shall we cross the river now
and rest in the shade of the trees?

Stonewall, dying, speaks thusly to his troops,
but the troops have vanished, they are
boycotting the river, they are
boycotting the shade of the trees,
they have boycotted the dying man's dream—
they are in a dark room waiting for the pieces
to surface. They are listening for silence,
but what they hear is the blood
making its way by their ears.

*

When I say my bed shall comfort me,
my couch shall ease my complaint,
then thou scarest me with dreams
and terrifiest me through visions.

Then Descartes, groping back toward God
in the God-filled room: *I think, hence* et-
cetera. But they called reason
good sense back then, and who can blame them,
God arriving at the doorstep just in time—
holding the puzzle's only missing piece.

Author of the voices in their heads.

I think, hence hence—hence
(. . . three centuries, four decades, nine years,
God only knows how many days, and counting . . .)
your voices are not your own,
you are nothing. Then *All poetry*
is a form of prayer—but that's Keats,
voice of a sacred century.

I do not think they understood that what
they were asking for, in the end, was
the image and the story of our bodies.
I do not think they believed
in how thoroughly we could love them.

*

That music in the background, trying to be
of use: it seems so strange to hear you say
in the course of a lifetime, over and over—
I've never been laid so low.
And that's the sound of the river
of blood in your head, laughing, saying
just put it back somehow together.

Century as the voices in our heads.
Mousetrap in the corner snapping NOW
in the backward-moving mind.
Imagine yesterday. Imagine
the sound of a horse eating acorns.

And what if the wind really is
moaning as it makes its way past our ears?
Can you live behind this soul?
Never stopping to think it.

That music in the background, trying again
to be of use—it's in the background, it's
trying to be of use. Well, here's to it,
and to the back turned toward the river—
the ending, some ending, somebody's ending.
We couldn't resist, we put this room in.
Here's to how we *had* to do it.

*

It is fall. Yesterday was Thursday.
You were right—remember, you said it
yourself, there's an edge beyond the edge
and it belongs to us. I would do anything
to pull you through. Anything
to pull through. Tule fog rising,
curling in the edges of the paper,
writing it down now—how you will rise
and go calmly to the kitchen, take down
the bowl. Looking for cereal. Looking for milk.

Listen.—I present these things in order
of appearance, not because that is the order
in which you must now make them happen
but because, as it happens—they can also
be arranged this way in order
to present a progression.

HOWEVER,

what if I said I wanted
myself back whole — what then?

"What's broken, we can fix,"
the humans would say — predictably.

You have to love them for that.

Of course, nothing *really* heals.

I know what the wind knows.
Tearing across the prairie,

bits of grit riding its cold storm —
grit like coal dust, or like ashes:

What's the difference?
There's enough love here.

THE SEVENTH REVELATION OF MY
THIRTY-SEVENTH YEAR

You can take it as a matter
of course: this matter of how
anything your attention falls on

means: *there's this again, that*
yours should be a rocky life —
nothing but scrapes and sighs

to steer by — : so that even if
you *were* the sort of person
to be stopped in your tracks

by tomatoes in a shop window —
vines still attached, vines
like wax, the flawless fruit

like a model for fruit — even if
you were, you'd take it
as a prophecy for your coming

arrest, get drunk, fall asleep
on the CamBus, and get arrested —
returning, upon your release,

through the unoccupied swirling
of the snow to your small
brown house on the floodplain —

or you could take this life,
so badly broken in, and say
instead, say, *I lay me down now*

like a lace of ripples
in sand, by the wild
and lovely Atlantic.

LACK, THE WILLOW

The good earth spins and circles.
    The *willow* speaks from the center.

The willow speaks with a record force.
    The warning is retrospective.

The universe raises the body.
    We respond with our lives.

We respond with our lives?
    Yes—I carry this feather wherever I go.

I thought that was interpretation.
    It is our lives.

Our minds make a wedge.
    The language is breaking.

You call the feather something else?
    Later, it will be my home.

Where the leaf trembles and the ant marches?
    Where my ghost will come home to rest.

Horses need a place to come home to, to drown.
    I carry this feather wherever I go.

The mind's a mysterious master.
    The world is a wedge.

Aren't we born with a light in our eyes?
    The mathematics of stars and planets.

Aren't we born with a storm in our brows?
    The willow is the record force.

The flat hands of moles pat the ground.
    Tunnel of fear, tunnel of grief.

Nothing can protect them?
    We have lost that argument.

Truth or innuendo?
    I carry this feather wherever I go.

The warning was retrospective.
    I carry the warning, I carry the feather.

Fear is a place to come home to, to drown?
    I carry this feather.

Respond with your grief.
    I respond with this feather.

The good earth spins in darkness?
    I carry this feather.

    I carry this feather wherever I go.

I HAVE BEEN LIVING

I have been living
closer to the ocean than I thought—
in a rocky cove thick with seaweed.

It pulls me down when I go wading.
Sometimes, to get back to land
takes everything that I have in me.

Sometimes, to get back to land
is the worst thing a person can do.
Meanwhile, we are dreaming:

The body is innocent.
She has never hurt me.
What we love flutters in us.

THE PRAIRIE AS VALID PROVIDER

1.

Occasionally, I start from scratch.

Scratch for me is the prairie
and moonlight is my favorite season —
white when it lies,
white when the rain pours over,
white when it doesn't.

I can hear the sheep crying
in the driving rain — lightning
catches the world as an image
might catch history.

Then the prairie goes on
a long way, and it looks
like the sheep are just grazing.

Rot enters the rolled hay.

2.

Stepping right over what I started to say—
there's the *ha ha* of it.
Not this pit of my personal making
but *our* pit.

Not how when the city I love
shook itself down,
the bodies in the highway sandwich
smelled for days—
but how the kids in the mosh pit
kept on dancing.

Theirs is an informed despair—
it's all sweat and bashing,

but when they rise up,
thin shadows in the bluish light,
and plunge back toward the field
of up-stretched arms—they know
those arms will catch them.

They know the crowd will hold them up
as long as it can.

Speaking strictly for myself here,
I'd say that that's a lot to know.

3.
It's true.
This is about love.

Could have been love
for the cryptic mysticness of happiness
as a thought.

But there was a man I loved
in that city.

Don't know how I ended up
back at scratch — on a green planet
watching the lightning,
mind like a minor civil division,
metabolism adrift and some
crucial parts missing.

The crocodile skull on the windowsill
is watching the prairie
for signs of change.

I am watching the croc
for signs of a name.

For a long time now
I have known
I was going someplace impossible —

I have known.

Olive, willow, memory. —

This is for the hypnotic jasmine
that grows outside my window.

4.

Exactly what kind of sleep
do you think you could use?

Like a flash for the world
to take shape in.

(This
is no place for contradictions.
No place for argument.)

I run water in the tub.
I turn off the lights
and light the floating candles.

When they sail under the leaky faucet
there's a hissing that could be
flesh burning, but isn't.

In the dark the voice continues —
Lie still my dear, sleep sweet.
(Might be something I read,
but it sounds like my guardian angel.)

Is everything all right?

No, but lie still all the same.

5.

I miss him
like the end of the world
at the end of the century.
In which nobody wrote *Fidelio*.

Enough to make you want
to explode a sentence?

Enough to make me.

But the sentences have all been exploded.
I checked.

Book, bookmark, bed—we shall now
empty one out: one sentence:

"I heard a child asking
where its legs were"
(By Grand Central Station
I Sat Down and Wept)

—and somewhere on a dark platform
a door opens on a history
and quickly slams shut.

And quickly slams shut?
And quickly slams shut.

As with "somewhere else
there was a bombing."

And somewhere else.
I can't tell you
the who and whom of it.
Can't even tell you the price
of the morning paper.

Just help me pull the bodies
out of the mud.

Grab that arm and drag. Good.

Now work a little faster.
This is not just any field.
This is a field of art.

6.

The moon and the sheep and the hay and the rain.

Once upon a time
there was a *once upon a time.*

Because I loved,
because I failed
came the space for greater sorrow.

What, if anything,
do we know?

How to make a bomb?
How to unmake a sentence?
How to rate a sorrow
on a scale from one to ten?

What the prairie said
was mercy the sky
refuses. Truth hovers
over the feasible landscape:

There is no god.
Loneliness is the lesser pain.

If I can be of use—call me.

7.

This is for the kids in the mosh pit.
Lie still my dears, sleep sweet.
The sentence the angels unraveled
the wind plays back as music.

Angels? What angels?

Play that back as music.

The music in the mosh pit's
hard enough to make you think of hate.

And when you listen to the words?

When lightning flashes on the prairie
it's gold all over green — all over.

And when you listen to the words?

O.K. — *when you listen to the words*
you know that they want life
just like we did, only harder.

Play that back as music.

Really the grass has tufts of white?

And the jasmine has yellow flowers.

114

"Rather" is for Randall Potts.

"Talking to You" is for Julie Checkoway Thomsen.

"Notes toward a Definition" includes quotes from or references to the following individuals and texts: Baudelaire, the Book of Job, Stonewall Jackson, John Keats, and Paul Simon.

"The Ring around the Reappearing Body": The story about Patrick is recounted in *Necessary Loses* by Judith Viorst. The words attributed to this true child are a direct quote. *GVW, in memoriam.*

"House of Poured-Out Waters": "House of olives," "house of mercy," and "house of poured-out waters" are different translations of Bethez, Bethesda, or Bethzatha—the pool in Jerusalem where Jesus is said to have healed a man who had been sick for thirty-eight years. "Nimitz" refers to the Nimitz Freeway, which collapsed in San Francisco's October 1989 earthquake, killing forty-two motorists. "Lisa" and "Hedda" are references to the 1988 New York City case in which Joel Steinberg was convicted of first-degree manslaughter in the beating death of his illegally adopted "daughter" Lisa, who was six at the time. Hedda Nussbaum was his partner, who had also been beaten by Steinberg. Lisa was buried in New York; her gravestone reads "GOD'S ANGEL." The italicized phrases on 78 are quotes from the Book of Job.

"The Prairie as Valid Provider": In the fifth section, *"By Grand Central Station I Sat Down and Wept"* is a reference to the book by that title, by Elizabeth Smart, from which the preceding two lines are a direct quote.

ILLINOIS POETRY SERIES

Laurence Lieberman, Editor

The American Book of the Dead
Jim Barnes (1982)

The Floating Candles
Sydney Lea (1982)

Northbook
Frederick Morgan (1982)

Collected Poems, 1930–83
Josephine Miles (1983; reissue,
1999)

The River Painter
Emily Grosholz (1984)

Healing Song for the Inner Ear
Michael S. Harper (1984)

The Passion of the Right-Angled
Man
T. R. Hummer (1984)

Dear John, Dear Coltrane
Michael S. Harper (1985)

Poems from the Sangamon
John Knoepfle (1985)

In It
Stephen Berg (1986)

The Ghosts of Who We Were
Phyllis Thompson (1986)

Moon in a Mason Jar
Robert Wrigley (1986)

Lower-Class Heresy
T. R. Hummer (1987)

Poems: New and Selected
Frederick Morgan (1987)

Furnace Harbor: A Rhapsody of
the North Country
Philip D. Church (1988)

Bad Girl, with Hawk
Nance Van Winckel (1988)

Blue Tango
Michael Van Walleghen (1989)

Eden
Dennis Schmitz (1989)

Waiting for Poppa at the
Smithtown Diner
Peter Serchuk (1990)

Great Blue
Brendan Galvin (1990)

What My Father Believed
Robert Wrigley (1991)

Something Grazes Our Hair
S. J. Marks (1991)

Walking the Blind Dog
G. E. Murray (1992)

The Sawdust War
Jim Barnes (1992)

The God of Indeterminacy
Sandra McPherson (1993)

Off-Season at the Edge of the
World
Debora Greger (1994)

The Silent Singer: New and
Selected Poems
Len Roberts (2001)

The Salt Hour
J. P. White (2001)

NATIONAL POETRY SERIES

Eroding Witness
Nathaniel Mackey (1985)
Selected by Michael S. Harper

Palladium
Alice Fulton (1986)
Selected by Mark Strand

Cities in Motion
Sylvia Moss (1987)
Selected by Derek Walcott

The Hand of God and a Few
Bright Flowers
William Olsen (1988)
Selected by David Wagoner

The Great Bird of Love
Paul Zimmer (1989)
Selected by William Stafford

Stubborn
Roland Flint (1990)
Selected by Dave Smith

The Surface
Laura Mullen (1991)
Selected by C. K. Williams

The Dig
Lynn Emanuel (1992)
Selected by Gerald Stern

My Alexandria
Mark Doty (1993)
Selected by Philip Levine

The High Road to Taos
Martin Edmunds (1994)
Selected by Donald Hall

Theater of Animals
Samn Stockwell (1995)
Selected by Louise Glück

The Broken World
Marcus Cafagña (1996)
Selected by Yusef Komunyakaa

Nine Skies
A. V. Christie (1997)
Selected by Sandra McPherson

Lost Wax
Heather Ramsdell (1998)
Selected by James Tate

So Often the Pitcher Goes to
Water until It Breaks
Rigoberto González (1999)
Selected by Ai

Renunciation
Corey Marks (2000)
Selected by Philip Levine

OTHER POETRY VOLUMES

Local Men and Domains
James Whitehead (1987)

Her Soul beneath the Bone:
Women's Poetry on Breast
Cancer
Edited by Leatrice Lifshitz (1988)

Days from a Dream Almanac
Dennis Tedlock (1990)

Working Classics: Poems on
Industrial Life
Edited by Peter Oresick and
Nicholas Coles (1990)

Hummers, Knucklers, and Slow
Curves: Contemporary Baseball
Poems
Edited by Don Johnson (1991)

The Double Reckoning of
Christopher Columbus
Barbara Helfgott Hyett (1992)

Selected Poems
Jean Garrigue (1992)

New and Selected Poems,
1962–92
Laurence Lieberman (1993)

The Dig and Hotel Fiesta
Lynn Emanuel (1994)

For a Living: The Poetry of Work
Edited by Nicholas Coles and
Peter Oresick (1995)

The Tracks We Leave: Poems on
Endangered Wildlife of North
America
Barbara Helfgott Hyett (1996)

Peasants Wake for Fellini's
Casanova and Other Poems
Andrea Zanzotto; edited and
translated by John P. Welle and
Ruth Feldman; drawings by
Federico Fellini and Augusto
Murer (1997)

Moon in a Mason Jar and What
My Father Believed
Robert Wrigley (1997)

The Wild Card: Selected Poems,
Early and Late
Karl Shapiro; edited by Stanley
Kunitz and David Ignatow
(1998)

Turtle, Swan and Bethlehem in
Broad Daylight
Mark Doty (2000)

Typeset in 10/14 Electra
with Nofret display
Designed by Cope Cumpston
Composed by Jim Proefrock
at the University of Illinois Press
Manufactured by Cushing-Malloy, Inc.

University of Illinois Press
1325 South Oak Street
Champaign, IL 61820-6903
www.press.uillinois.edu